Which Side Is Up?

Cartoons from *Daily Maverick*

Acknowledgements: Thanks to my editors at Daily Maverick (Branko Brkic and Marianne Thamm) for many light bulb moments and thanks to all production staff; Mike Wills for the write stuff; my assistant Eleanora Bresler for smooth runnings; Bridget Impey and all at Jacana; Claudine Willatt-Bate for layout; and the Zaprock home team – Nomalizo Ndlazi and my family, Karina, Tevya and Nina.

10 Orange Street
Sunnyside
Auckland Park 2092
South Africa
(+27 11) 628 3200
www.jacana.co.za

in association with

© Jonathan Shapiro, 2019

All rights reserved.

ISBN 978-1-4314-2939-4

Cover design by Jonathan Shapiro
Page layout by Claudine Willatt-Bate
Job no. 003635

Printed and bound by ABC Press, Cape Town

See a complete list of Jacana titles at www.jacana.co.za
See Zapiro's list and archive at www.zapiro.com

For inquiring minds

ZAPIRO annuals
The Madiba Years (1996)
The Hole Truth (1997)
End of Part One (1998)
Call Mr Delivery (1999)
The Devil Made Me Do It! (2000)
The ANC Went in 4x4 (2001)
Bushwhacked (2002)
Dr Do-Little and the African Potato (2003)
Long Walk to Free Time (2004)
Is There a Spin Doctor In the House? (2005)
Da Zuma Code (2006)
Take Two Veg and Call Me In the Morning (2007)
Pirates of Polokwane (2008)
Don't Mess With the President's Head (2009)
Do You Know Who I Am?! (2010)
The Last Sushi (2011)
But Will It Stand Up In Court? (2012)
My Big Fat Gupta Wedding (2013)
It's Code Red! (2014)
Rhodes Rage (2015)
Dead President Walking (2016)
Hasta la Gupta, baby! (2017)
Let the Sunshine In (2018)

Other books
The Mandela Files (2008)
VuvuzelaNation (2013)
DemoCrazy (2014)
WTF: capturing Zuma – a cartoonist's tale (2018)

3 October 2018

ANC secretary-general Ace Magashule's been meeting secretly to scheme with former president Zuma against President Ramaphosa

Finance minister Nhlanhla Nene tells the Zondo Commission of Inquiry into State Capture that Zuma and cabinet ministers pressured him in 2015 to sign a potentially crippling nuclear deal with Russia. He refused.

4 October 2018

Next thing at the inquiry: he admits to a series of meetings with the Guptas that he'd previously denied having. And then resigns.

9 October 2018

11 October 2018

Tito Mboweni – former Reserve Bank governor, prolific tweeter and subject of a popular Cassper Nyovest rap song – is Nene's surprise replacement

7 October 2018 — Selected by the US president for the Supreme Court, Justice Brett Kavanaugh is confirmed by the Senate despite accusations of sexual assault and bizarre testimony about beer drinking

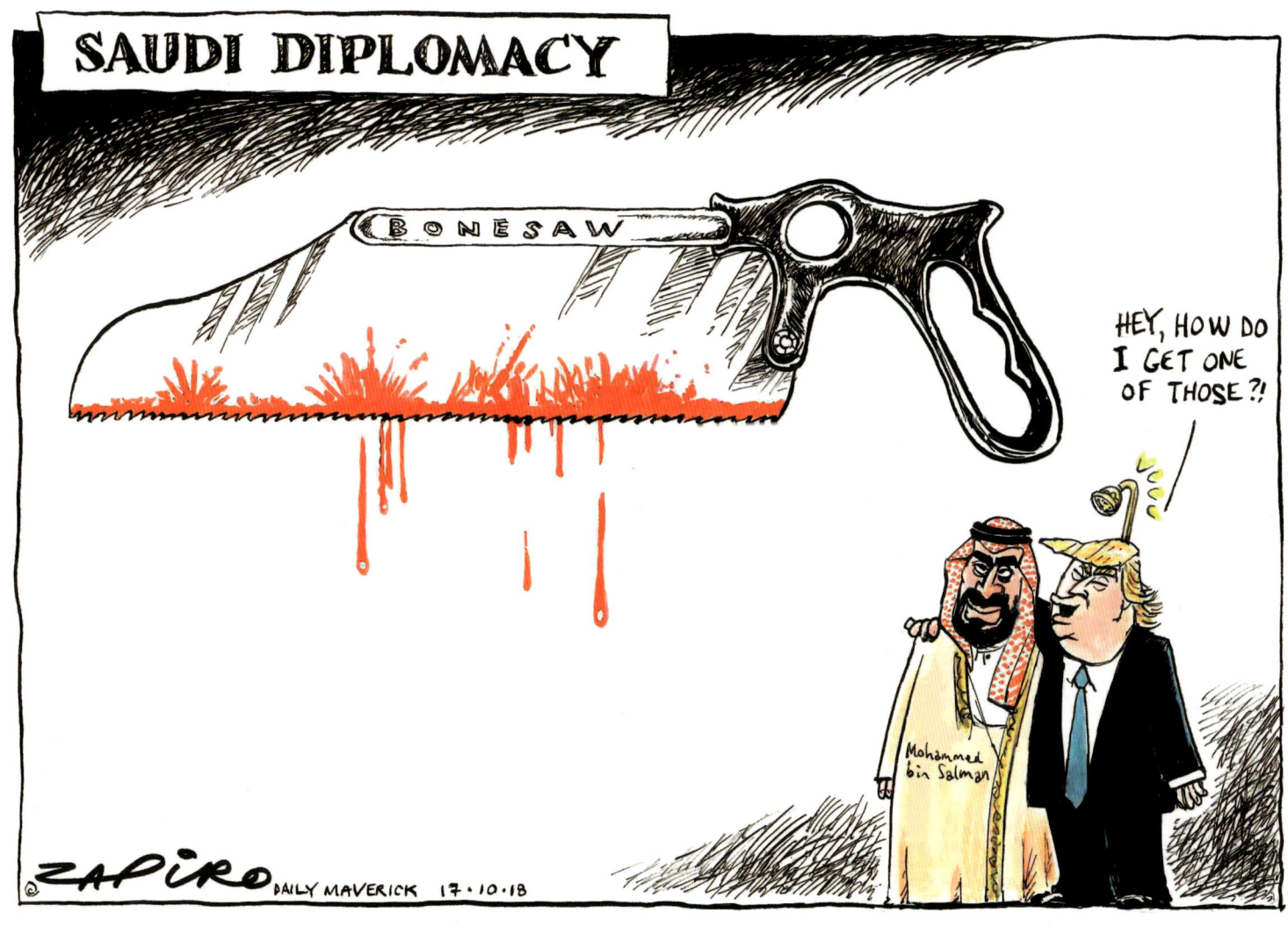

17 October 2018 — Dissident Saudi journalist Jamal Khashoggi is lured to a Saudi consulate where he is murdered and hacked to pieces. The kingdom's Crown Prince, a key Trump ally, is directly implicated.

A damning investigative report implicates the EFF in the criminal looting of VBS Bank. R16m in 'gratuitous payments' went to the brother of party deputy Floyd Shivambu.

12 October 2018

In response, Shivambu and EFF leader Julius Malema attack public enterprises minister Pravin Gordhan with plot theories and denials

23 October 2018

Justice Robert Nugent recommends that the president fire SARS boss (and Zuma crony) Tom Moyane for crippling management and eroding tax collection

18 October 2018

Nigerian evangelical pastor Timothy Omotoso is on trial for rape and human trafficking. There's outrage at his advocate's brutal treatment of a brave accuser.

22 October 2018

24 October 2018 — New finance minister's first major speech after just two weeks in office

26 October 2018 — Explosive devices sent to well-known targets of American right-wing vitriol

Gupta-linked home affairs minister Malusi Gigaba apologises for a lewd cellphone video he says he intended for his wife but which is being used to blackmail him

30 October 2018

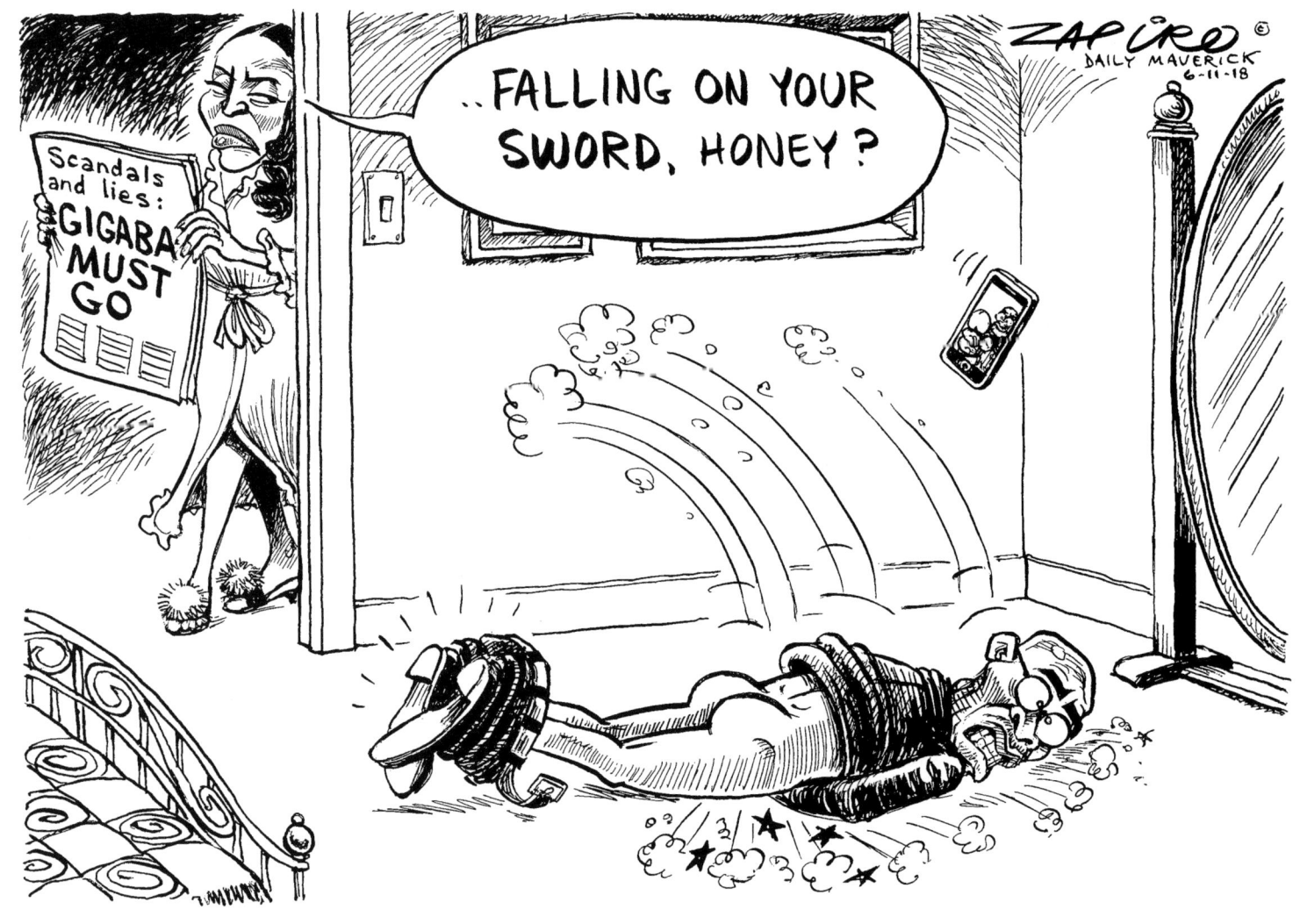

6 November 2018

Increased clamour for Gigaba's sacking after he's denied leave to appeal against a damning judgment that he had lied and violated the Constitution

After a drawn-out squabble, Patricia de Lille finally resigns as mayor of Cape Town and from the DA. She says Mmusi Maimane's party is abusive and she'll continue legal actions to clear her name.

31 October 2018

Two bad eggs remain senior provincial leaders despite an integrity committee thumbs-down. Hlongwa is under investigation over massive kickbacks while Mahlangu was responsible for the Life Esidimeni tragedy which cost 144 lives.

2 November 2018

7 November 2018 — In crucial midterm elections, Trump drives a divisive anti-immigrant campaign

8 November 2018 — A mixed result – the president tweets about a great triumph in the Senate but the #MeToo wave and anger at his sexism sweep a record number of women into Congress

Gordhan to testify at the Zondo Commission while facing a subpoena from the public protector, wild EFF criticism and corruption allegations from the previously unknown Academic and Professional Staff Association

13 November 2018

Detailing 'the forces of greed' behind State Capture and behind Zuma/Gupta crony appointments like Dudu Myeni as SAA chair and Tom Moyane as SARS boss

21 November 2018

The president told parliament his ANC leadership campaign got no funding from tainted facilities management company Bosasa. Later he admits money was received.

20 November 2018

15 November 2018 — Iconic co-creator of many Marvel superheroes

British PM Theresa May cannot get her Brexit plan past parliament.
Anarchic artist Banksy's 'Girl with Balloon' recently 'self-shredded' during its sale at auction.

Ramaphosa reshuffles his cabinet. Nomvula Mokonyane and Bathabile Dlamini are disturbing survivors in new ministries.

27 November 2018 — More Malema rabble-rousing, this time addressing a crowd outside the Zondo Inquiry

Former government spin doctor and Gupta media owner, Mzwanele Manyi, begins smoothly in front of Zondo but is dismantled under questioning

28 November 2018

5 December 2018 — Shamila Batohi becomes the National Prosecuting Authority's sixth new boss in seven years

7 December 2018 — All of Batohi's experience and credibility may not be enough

11 December 2018

The NPA has charged former ANC Western Cape leader Marius Fransman with the sexual assault of a young party employee. Now ANC spokesman Pule Mabe faces allegations from a Luthuli House worker.

12 December 2018

High Court rules Zuma will no longer receive state funding for his corruption trial defence
and that the state must take legal steps to recover taxpayers' money already spent

14 December 2018

21 December 2018

Mzwanele Manyi joins the newly-formed African Transformation Movement to contest elections, saying 'if the Guptas give me money I will take it'

14 January 2019

15 January 2019 — Debt-ridden power supplier wants 15% annual price increases for the next three years

Protests erupt in Zimbabwe after President Emmerson Mnangagwa announces a tripling of the petrol price

16 January 2019

Zondo Inquiry's star witness: Bosasa's former operations chief, Angelo Agrizzi, turns against the company and his old boss, Gavin Watson, with exhaustive evidence of bribery and corruption

Agrizzi details how hefty bribes to key officials gained lucrative government contracts, especially in the prisons department

23 January 2019

25 January 2019 — Named and nicknamed – Agrizzi says Bosasa got the NPA to shut down investigations by paying off then deputy national director Nomgcobo Jiba and special director Lawrence Mrwebi

22 January 2019

Facebook's 'ten-year challenge' meme is all the rage as rumours surface of the Zuma faction's win-at-all-costs fightback

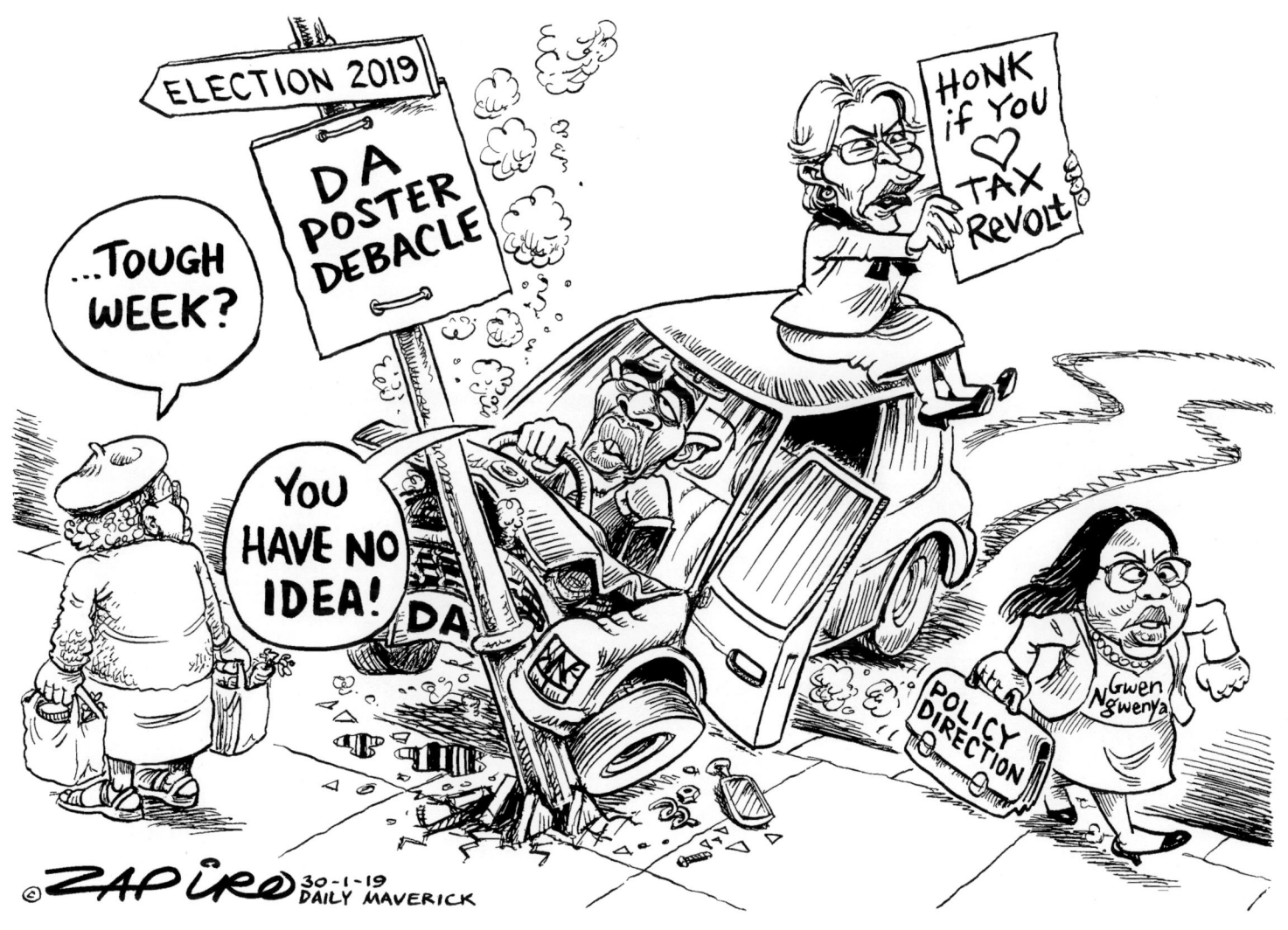

Maimane's under pressure – cringeworthy election posters, former leader Helen Zille touting a tax revolt and his policy head resigns citing lack of support

Another Bosasa executive, Andries van Tonder, tells the Zondo Inquiry that the word 'chicken' was company code for corruption − 'one ton of chicken represented R1m'

1 February 2019

7 February 2019 — The annual SONA showpiece

11 February 2019 — After SONA, EFF MP Marshall Dlamini assaults a member of parliamentary security. The party claims this was defence against a plot by elite police and right-wing groups to kill Julius Malema.

13 February 2019 — Return of load shedding

14 February 2019

19 February 2019   Mboweni's first budget is a harsh reality check

17 February 2019

Congress of the People leader Mosiuoa Lekota stuns parliament with an allegation that Ramaphosa had worked with the Security Branch in the apartheid era

After Angelo Agrizzi's devastating testimony, Bosasa (now known as African Global Operations) goes into liquidation. The company blames 'negative media reports'.

20 February 2019

Loss-making South African Airways is to be split into three parts – domestic, regional and international

ANC deputy secretary-general Jessie Duarte confirms rape allegations have been made against presidential spokesman Zizi Kodwa

Viral video shows a pastor in Gauteng performing a miraculous 'resurrection' of a dead man during a church service

27 February 2019

Evidence mounting at the Mokgoro Inquiry into the fitness of suspended NPA heavyweights Nomgcobo Jiba and Lawrence Mrwebi to hold office

1 March 2019

A senior SAA pilot is forced to resign after flying unlicensed for 20 years. The Zondo Inquiry hears that former SAA chair – and Zuma favourite – Dudu Myeni leaked NPA files to Bosasa's Gavin Watson.

5 March 2019

A widely-shared livestream video shows singer Mandla 'Mampintsha' Maphumulo assaulting his girlfriend Bongekile 'Babes Wodumo' Simelane

It's a standard EFF tactic – brutal social media trolling of critics.
This time journalist Karima Brown is threatened with rape and violence.

10 March 2019

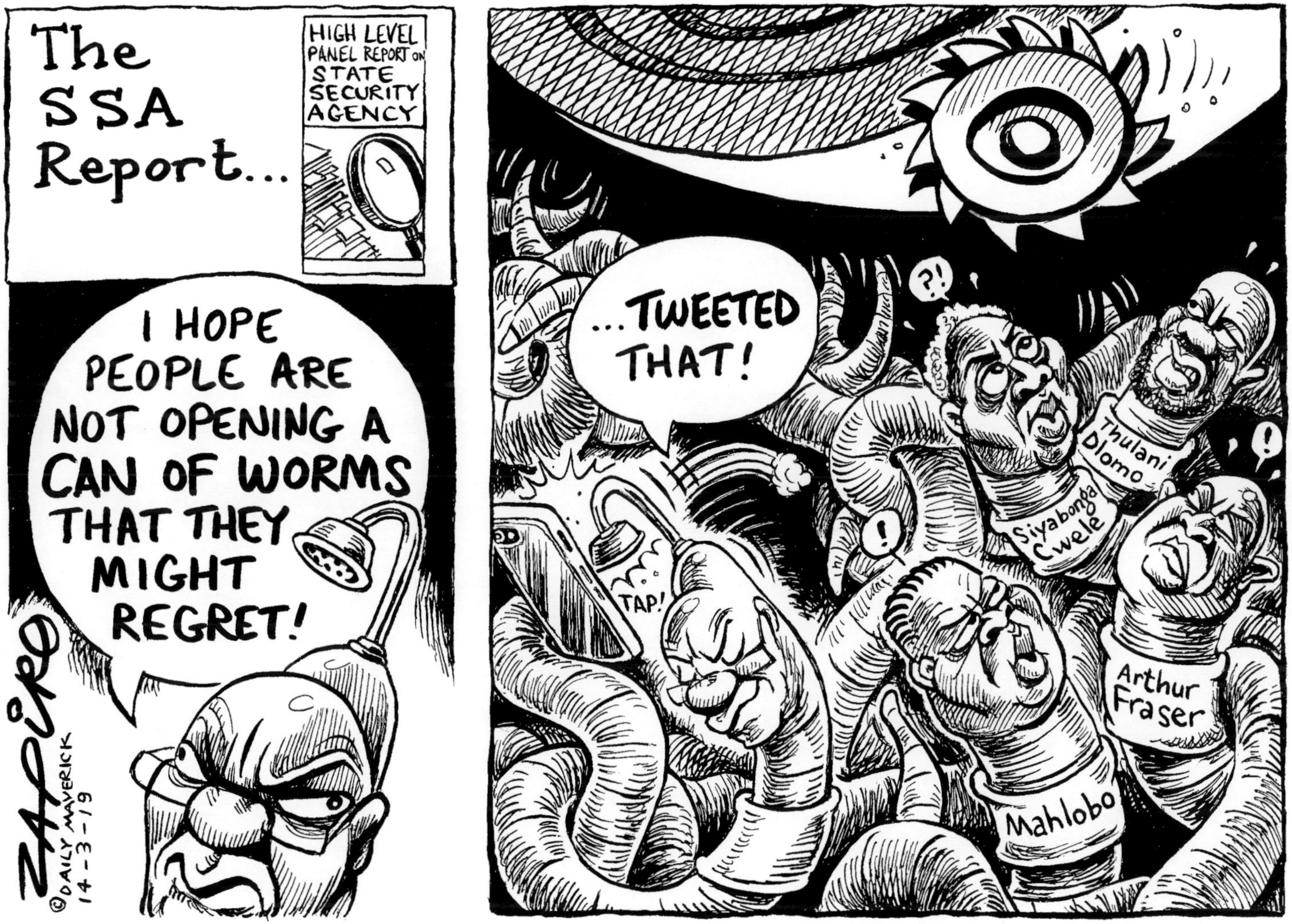

Zuma's veiled threat on social media after findings that he and former ministers and top officials abused the State Security Agency for political interests

15 March 2019 — The party's list of potential MPs is littered with names implicated in State Capture and corruption

18 March 2019 — British Prime Minister Theresa May ploughs on with Brexit after yet another defeat in parliament

19 March 2019

Terrorism shatters peaceful New Zealand when fifty are killed at two Christchurch mosques by a racist gunman

21 March 2019 — Announcement that a crack team of engineers is on the case

Load shedding disrupts the public holiday

Gangster State, a new book by journalist Pieter-Louis Myburgh, details the corruption network under ANC secretary-general Ace Magashule when he was Free State premier

3 April 2019

The president's own Bosasa scandal grows when it's revealed that his son received monthly advisory fees totalling R2m

28 March 2019

1 April 2019

The disastrous Tom Moyane era at the SA Revenue Service is over.
Respected former deputy commissioner Edward Kieswetter is the new boss.

She has a history of run-ins with reporters.
This time the deputy secretary-general lashes out at an eNCA journalist.

At the inquiry into controversial dealings by the Public Investment Corporation, Independent Newspapers' boss Dr Iqbal Survé grandiosely defends himself, claiming negative propaganda scuppered his deal with the PIC to list his Sagamartha Technologies at a vastly inflated price

7 April 2019

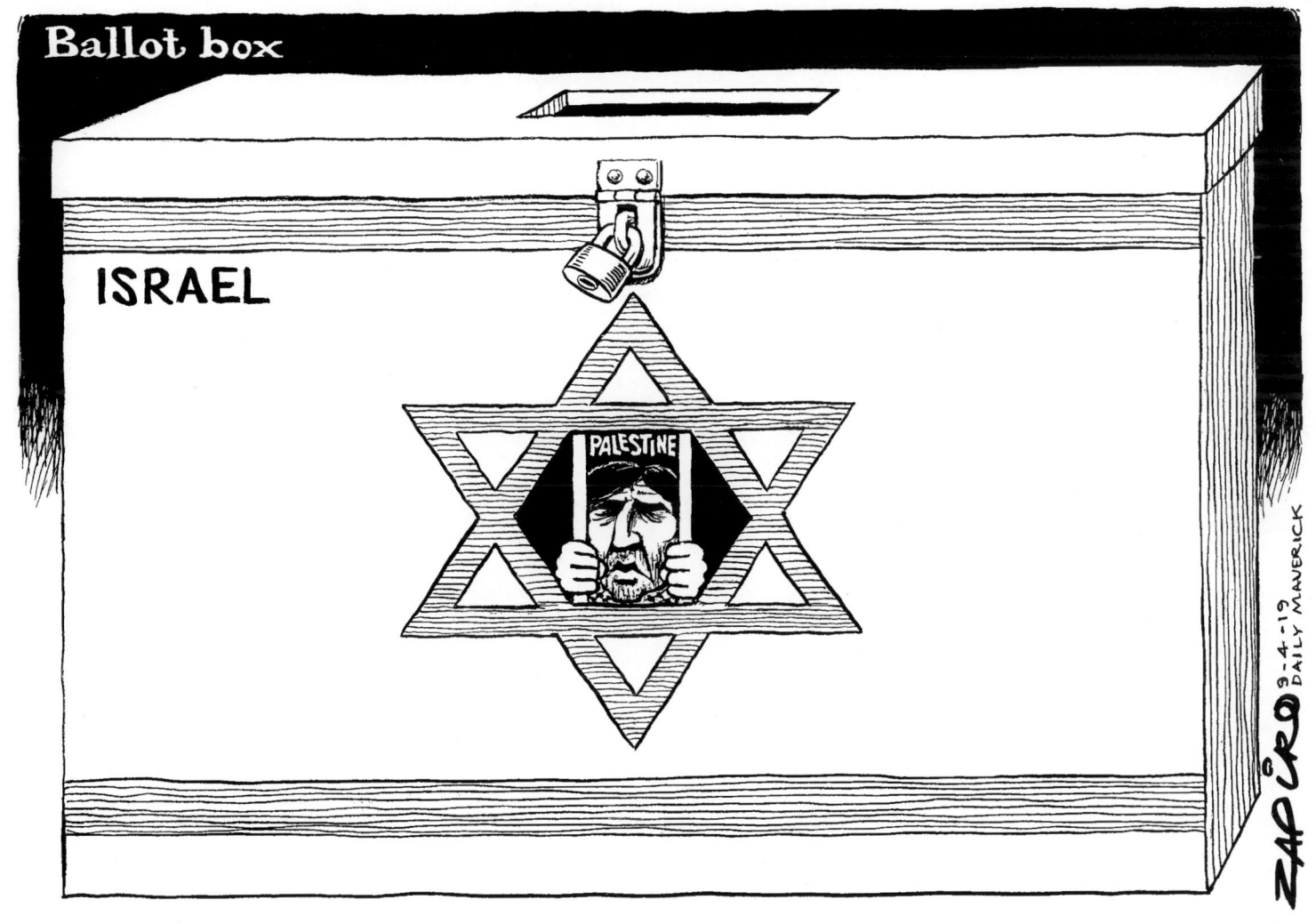

Israel goes to the polls. Prime minister Benjamin Netanyahu pledges to annex settlements in the occupied West Bank if he wins.

9 April 2019

10 April 2019

Strange reports that the president was asked by Libyan authorities to help recover a fortune stashed by now-deceased dictator Muammar Gaddafi at Zuma's Nkandla home

ANC Youth League members violently force the cancellation of a launch event for *Gangster State* and they say they'll publicly burn copies

16 April 2019

Eleven turbulent and injury-stricken years after his last major win, Tiger Woods takes the Masters

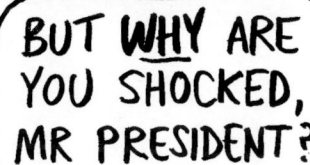

The president's refrain

24 April 2019 — 290 killed in multiple attacks on churches and hotels in Sri Lanka. An obscure Islamist group is blamed.

The story of a rogue unit at SARS under Pravin Gordhan has long been discredited as a smear by pro-Zuma spooks. Yet the public protector probes Gordhan again based on one EFF complaint.

25 April 2019

26 April 2019 — More than 50 die in devastating floods and storms sweeping KZN during the election campaign

Freedom Day – celebrating 25 years of democracy

1 May 2019 — More extreme weather lashes the south and east of the continent

3 May 2019 — World Press Freedom Day

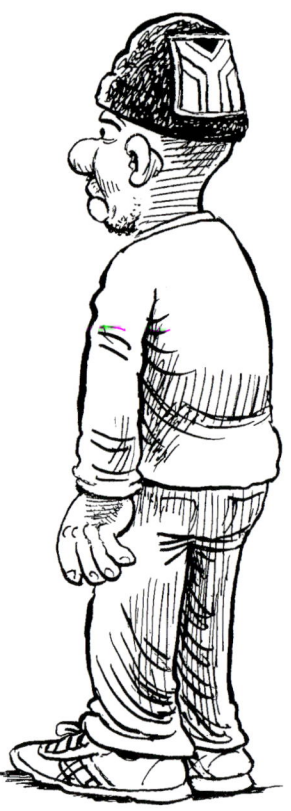

7 May 2019 — A choice of 48 parties on polling day

Admin glitches galore − stations not opening, ballot paper shortages, voters' rolls not checked to prevent duplicate voting and indelible ink that washes off nails

10 May 2019

14 May 2019 — The ANC drops below 60% nationally for the first time

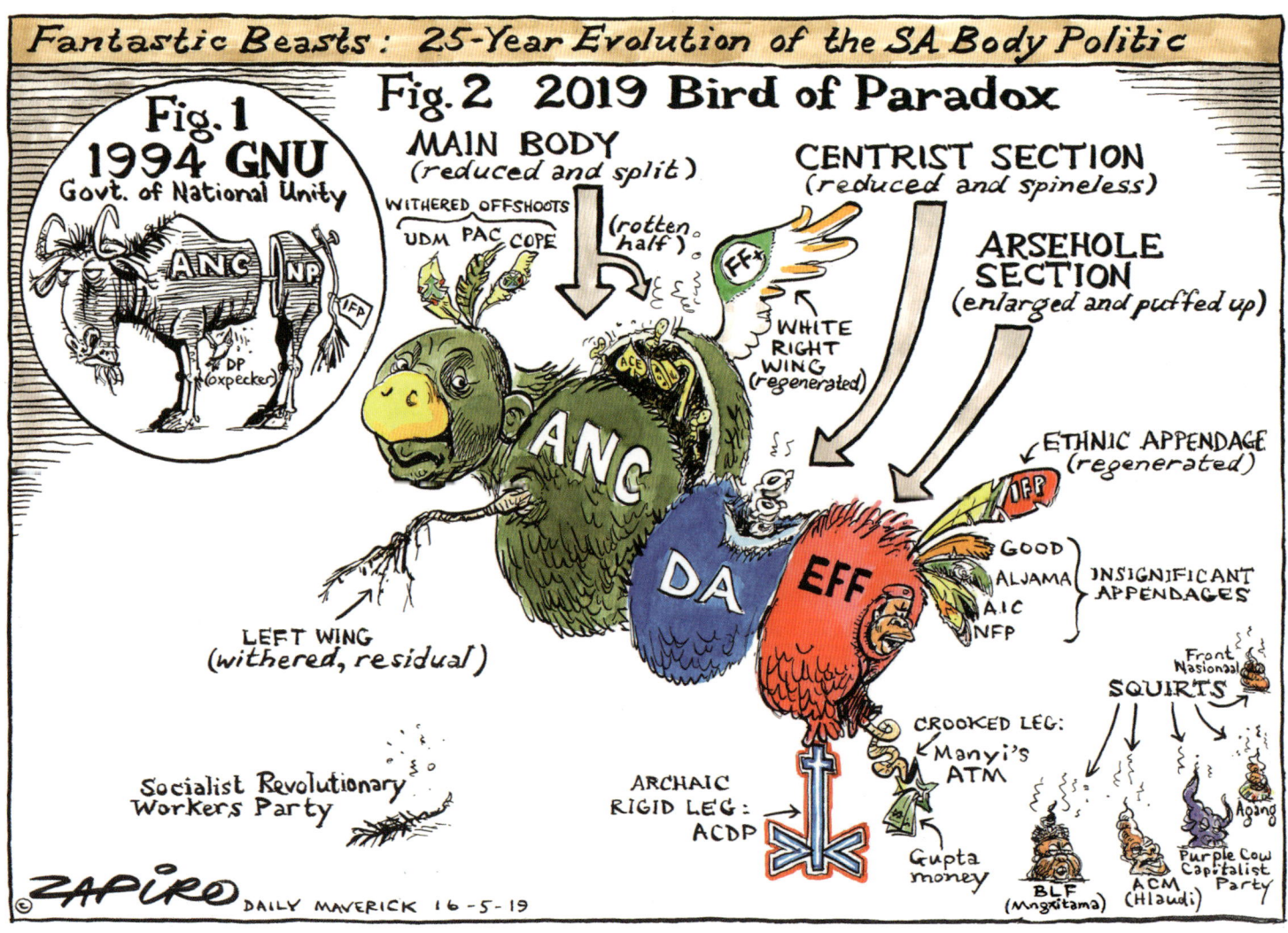

16 May 2019

17 May 2019

Admitting it was wrong to take campaign funding from Survé while there's an inquiry into his dealings with the PIC, the ANC returns the money

The public protector's latest legal hammering is a High Court ruling that she blatantly disregarded her constitutional duties or didn't understand them in her investigation into the Gupta-linked Estina farm scandal

22 May 2019

Surprise as ANC deputy president David 'The Cat' Mabuza postpones his swearing-in as an MP after a key committee finds he brought the party into disrepute

23 May 2019

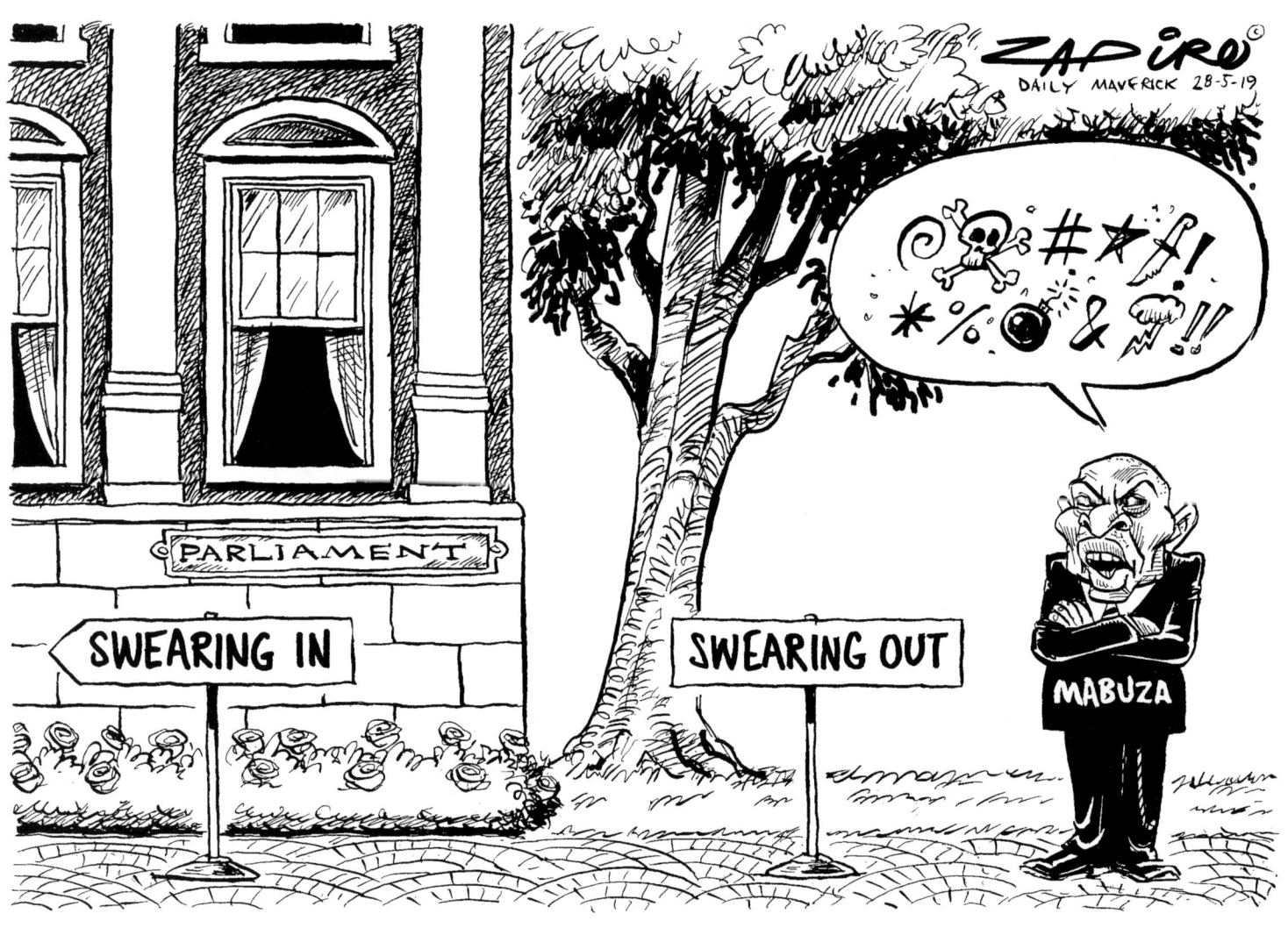

28 May 2019

30 May 2019

Mabuza's played a clever game – he faces down the integrity committee and returns to office emboldened

Back in court seeking a permanent stay of prosecution.
Members of his family also have legal troubles.

24 May 2019

Pravin Gordhan calls the public protector's latest report on him 'stunningly incompetent', saying she is part of a long fightback against those exposing State Capture

29 May 2019

Raymond Louw, former editor and champion of press freedom, dies at 92
(*Tribute cartoon drawn in 2016 and reprinted after his death*)

5 June 2019

Another institution to capture? Ace wants to change the Reserve Bank's mandate and use bond buybacks known as quantitative easing (which he calls 'quantity easing') to deal with national debt. The party soon disowns the statement.

6 June 2019

Sudanese despot Omar al-Bashir was ousted by the military who promised elections.
Two months later, they postpone the ballot and crack down on protestors, killing more than 100.

9 June 2019

11 June 2019

Deluded claim by the public protector. She was of course appointed by the former president who's complaining that he's run out of money to pay his legal fees.

The former social development minister finally resigns as an MP. In 2018 the Constitutional Court found her grossly negligent and said the NPA should consider laying charges.

12 June 2019

The ANC is investigating Magashule's alleged role in the formation of the rival African Transformation Movement

18 June 2019

The EFF keeps losing court cases and carrying costs – it owes Afrikaner lobby group AfriForum R550 000

The election means a second SONA for the year. The president talks of bullet trains, a hi-tech economy and a new futuristic city.

It's Ace's doing – a crew of discredited figures from the Zuma era get appointed to head parliamentary committees

25 June 2019

Eventually agreeing to appear before the Zondo Commission, Zuma's still trying to get the questions in advance and giving no guarantee he'll answer any of them

26 June 2019

30 June 2019 — Long-serving SANDF officer faces dismissal for wearing her hijab

Survé threatens another lawsuit – now against a highly respected, veteran labour journalist

4 July 2019

Rummaging through the trash outside a Camps Bay mansion, *Daily Maverick* reporter Marianne Thamm finds evidence of hypocritical high-living by EFF members attending SONA

6 July 2019 — PP's next wonky finding against Gordhan (which he duly challenges)

9 July 2019

High-profile Twitter war inside the ANC – the finance minister says e-tolls must stay and be paid while Gauteng premier David Makhura wants them scrapped

Bumbling evidence from former chief of protocol Bruce Koloane,
the fall guy for the scandal over the Gupta wedding plane which landed at
Waterkloof airforce base in 2013. He later became ambassador to the Netherlands.

11 July 2019

15 July 2019

His opening statement is a messy conspiracy theory about three decades of attempts on his life. He threatens to expose those who've sought to discredit him, naming former comrades like Ngoako Ramatlhodi (whom he himself had appointed to Cabinet!) as agents of the apartheid regime.

16 July 2019

19 July 2019 — Responding to detailed questions, it's a different story – he doesn't know or can't recall

18 July 2019

23 July 2019

The Constitutional Court agrees that the public protector's ABSA/Bankorp report was biased and that she lied to the lower court. And she is personally liable for 15% of the legal costs.

24 July 2019   Boris Johnson becomes UK prime minister

30 July 2019   Now the High Court finds her remedial orders against Gordhan to be vague and nonsensical

1 August 2019 — Stats SA releases alarming unemployment figures

5 August 2019 — A debt so vast that it's threatening to destabilise the entire economy

7 August 2019

Five mass shootings in eight days in the US. The president who won't act on gun control tweets concern as usual and is defended by his aides.

12 August 2019 — National Women's Day

14 August 2019 — Hong Kong's pro-democracy protestors disrupt the city's airport

Widows and unions say nothing's changed at Marikana since police gunned down 34 miners in 2012

16 August 2019

19 August 2019

Leaked e-mails reveal more compromising details about fundraising for Ramaphosa's 2017 ANC presidential election campaign

The High Court sets aside the whitewash findings of the long and expensive inquiry into the Arms Deal reluctantly established by Zuma and run by retired judge Willie Seriti

22 August 2019

26 August 2019 — Bosasa boss Gavin Watson, named at the Zondo Inquiry as a major briber of political figures, dies in a mysterious, high-speed, early morning crash at OR Tambo Airport

Brazilian president Jair Bolsanaro faces widespread international condemnation over the catastrophic burning of the Amazon rainforest. His friend Donald Trump defends him.

28 August 2019

31 August 2019

Suspended over a corrupt Durban Solid Waste contract, the city's ANC mayor eventually agrees to resign. She then changes her tune and returns to office.

August – nominally Women's Month – has seen UCT student Uyinene Mrwetyana and SA boxing champion Leighandre Jegels become the latest high-profile victims of gender-based violence

4 September 2019

3 September 2019 — Xenophobic violence in Johannesburg

Nigeria reacts

7 September 2019 — The former Zimbabwean president dies in a Singapore hospital

SA's Robbin' Hood

Armani, Gucci, Chivas Regal
Turns out Juju's all illegal
"Take from the rich for those in need!"
means steal from the poor to feed my greed.

11 September 2019

Daily Maverick/Scorpio report details how corrupt funds from the collapsed VBS Bank funded Malema's extravagant lifestyle

Refusing to give answers, the EFF gets in a froth when EWN reporter Barry Bateman is caught on tape calling Malema the p-word at a media conference

Hlaudi Motsoeneng, calamitous and unqualified boss of the Zuma-era SABC, brazens it out under questioning

13 September 2019

Hapless British prime minister likens himself to a superhero after losing yet another key Brexit vote

Chair of Old Mutual and former finance minister, Trevor Manuel, takes a swipe at a judge who ruled against the company in its ongoing legal battle to remove CEO Peter Moyo

20 September 2019

At the UN, Swedish 16-year-old Greta Thunberg
confronts politicians and business leaders on climate change

Embarrassments aplenty – Maimane drove an SUV 'donated' by Steinhoff's Markus Jooste, Malema's VBS doo-doo deepens and Zondo Inquiry hears that journo Ranjeni Munusamy and former top cop Bheki Cele got dirty funding

3 October 2019

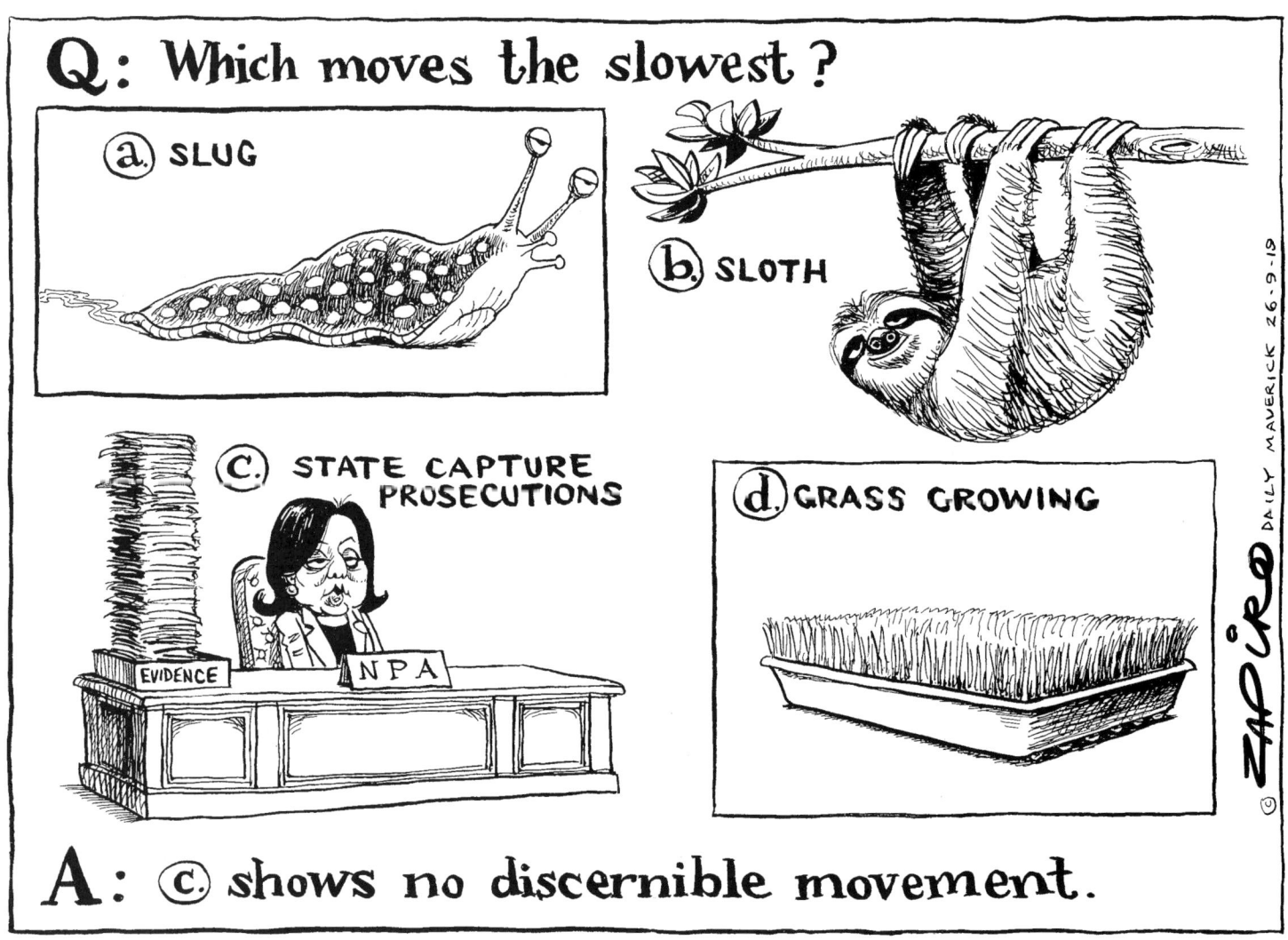

6 October 2019

Final straw, even for the Republicans? Congress initiates impeachment after a whistle-blower reveals Trump leaned on the Ukrainian president to dig up dirt on his Democrat rival Joe Biden.

22 September 2019   SABC can't afford screening rights